WHO AM I TO GOD
AND WHY DOES HE LOVE ME?

Robert Saunders

Book Writer Press

Who Am I to God and Why Does He Love Me?
Copyright © Robert Saunders 2015

ISBN: 0692500286 | 978-0692500286

Forward

Robert Saunders is a true miracle of God. I am also proud to call him my husband and best friend. Robert writes with such passion that it spills out of nearly every word on the page.

The book you hold in your hand is an awesome testament to the power of God. This story was written from the perspective of a man who found true freedom. It is the story of a traumatic childhood and a journey. Most importantly though is how God heals beyond belief. This story is based on Robert's life experience and how God really shows up in our everyday life

Thank you for taking the time to read this book, and it is my prayer that somehow you will see the awesomeness of God and that will draw you closer to Him.

Be blessed,
Jackie Saunders

A note from the author

As a former director of the Lazarus Transformation Center, I found I was being asked the question, "Who am I to God and why does He love me?" These questions were asked by men who suffer from low self-esteem, a variety of addictions, afflictions, and life controlling issues. I asked myself that same question many times after having an encounter with God. Once I discovered the answer, it helped me to reconcile in my mind that a terrible and even an evil person could be loved by God. Not only can a person be loved but also restored to sanity through intimacy with the creator God.

One thing is for certain, we do not go after God first. The Bible says clearly that no one comes to Jesus unless they are drawn by God the Father. God demonstrates His mercy and love toward us by drawing us to Himself while we are still a sinner. God doesn't want his children to be separated from Him. He knows that we are corrupted and without the strength or knowledge to seek Him out on our own

With that in mind, it is my prayer for you to read on with an expectation of being encountered by the God who created you. He is a God who loves you with His entire being. The Bible tells us that, "God is love" (1 John 4: 8 & 16). How comforting it is to know that!

Chapter One

As we begin to answer the question, "Who am I to God and why does He love me," we must begin with the very basic and fundamental question of, "Why did God create man?" In Genesis chapter one, we discover that God did create man.

Then God said, "Let us make man in our image, in our likeness, and let them rule over the fish of the sea and the birds of the air, over the livestock, over all the earth, and over all the creatures that move along the ground." So God created man in his own image, in the image of God He created him; Male and female He created them. (Genesis 1: 26-27 NIV)

We know that God did in fact make man, but why? What was His motivation? To find that answer, we will have to go several thousand years beyond creation to the close of the first century. The Apostle John wrote in his first epistle, chapter four verses six and eight, "We are from God... God is love," and verse eight he says that..." God is love".

So, what about this "love"? In a class I took called, "Theology of Holiness" by Dr. Stephen Manley, a world evangelist of 50 plus years and a well-known writer who has saturated in the gospel of Matthew and Acts, stated that "love" in the original language was a noun speaking of a person. After further research, I discovered what he meant. Love is a person and His name is God.

Many of you reading this book know something of the attributes of God. We call them the Omni's of God: omnipresent, omniscience, and omnipotent, meaning that God is always present, all knowing, and all powerful. However, "love" is not an attribute. Love is God's nature; it is who He is.

In order to make the point clear, Dr. Manley used an illustration of a conversation between Love and God. Love said to God, "You love so much that you need a place to put your love, a way to really express yourself." In agreement with Love, God got busy creating a place to put His love. We call this place earth.

On earth, God created all sorts of living things like plants, trees, flowers, animals that crawl, those that walk, and the fish of various kinds to inhabit the waters. All these, God spoke into existence. He simply said, "Let there be..." and out of His mind appeared all these life forms. However, these life forms weren't where God would put His love. But "man", whoa, that was different! How different? Let's go back to the Scriptures to find our answer.

The Lord God formed the man from the dust of the ground and breathed into his nostrils the breath of life, and the man became a living being. (Genesis 2:7 NIV)

Wow, now that's personal. God didn't just speak man into existence. He got down into the dirt and formed the shape of man and breathed life into him, creating a living, breathing, and intelligible person - in other words, a living soul. This means that man has, "God's fingerprints all over him." God literally put Himself into mankind and man was to have relationship with God at the most intimate of levels. I picture the love of parents to the life they produced out of themselves in their children. I have heard countless stories of the things parents would do to protect their children, even sacrificing their own life for them. God is no different.

He gave Himself over to death on the cross of Calvary to rescue us from the death that would separate us from Him for all of eternity.

This proved to me that God is personal and interactive, not removed and unattainable. The Bible also says that, "God walked with man in the cool of the day," telling us even more about His inter-activeness. I started to become even more curious about who God is and what He could possibly see in me?

One of the things that I learned was to stop judging myself, putting aside my own self-assessment. The fact of the matter is, we are always more harsh on ourselves than other people would be and certainly way more than God is. I found that judging myself put limitations on my openness and willingness to see God as He truly is—the God and creator of my very being.

True, I had a lot of reservations about letting go of my opinion of self; somehow it just seemed right to continue to see myself as worthless and useless to anyone, especially to myself. Somehow, staying negative was easier and more comfortable. After studying some things about psychology, I found that staying negative and depressed was a safety zone for my emotions. In other words, I didn't have to expect much of myself or anyone else.

I want to take just a moment to encourage you to keep reading and praying, because, on the other side of this negative state is a glorious and wonderful freedom from the bondage of the enemy whose sole purpose is to destroy you and any hope you have for the future. Read how God sees your future.

> **For I know the plans I have for you, declares the Lord, plans to prosper you and not to harm you, plans to give you hope and a future. Then you will call upon me and come and pray to me, and I will listen to you. You will seek me and find me when you seek me with all your heart. I will be found by you. (Jeremiah 29:11-14 NIV)**

What a wonderful promise by God. The very person who created you said that He has a plan for your life and that it is good, full of hope, and prosperous. He goes on to tell us that no matter what, if we search for Him, we will find Him. Did you know that this is a promise? The Bible tells us in First Corinthians chapter 20 that, no matter how many promises God has made, they are "yes" in Christ.

Throughout the Bible, God has shown us great and many promises to assure us of the future plans He has for us. It is now up to us to take hold of them and put our trust in Him.

> **Trust in the Lord with all your heart. And lean not on your own understanding; in all your ways acknowledge him, and He will make your paths straight. (Proverbs 3: 5-6 NIV)**

There is a truth that rings loud and clear here. God is not asking us to understand or lean on our own strength or understanding in order to accomplish His will for our lives. However, we as humans, especially men, have been told from our childhood or even scolded into believing that we are responsible to do everything. In other words, we were taught to lean or count on our own strength and understanding. We now seem to find it very difficult to let go of self-sourcing and allow Jesus to source our lives.

Let us investigate why it is so hard. In a recent class of 14 men of various ages and backgrounds, I found several answers: fear of the unknown, trust issues, not sure what "letting go" means, and how does one really let go? First of all, those are all legitimate questions and God understands that we don't understand fully.

Fear of the unknown is one of my favorite questions to address because the only answer is "belief". **be·lief** (b¹-lJf') *n.* **1.** The mental act, condition, or habit of placing trust or confidence in another. **2.** Mental acceptance of and conviction in the truth, actuality, or validity of something. **3.** Something believed or accepted as true, especially a particular tenet or a body of tenets accepted by a group of persons. (American Heritage Dictionary)

How quick we are as people to accept the lies of Satan over the Truth of God. The fact is, we can no more see the lie than the truth. If I take someone at their word, it isn't because I can see the results of their actions before they complete them. I simply believe they will do it. So why do we not trust God the same way?

When posing this question to a group of men, who don't even trust themselves let alone anyone else, especially God who they claim they can't see, the responses were varied. One discussion went as follows: "Well, if I can see into a man's eye then I'll know if he is lying to me, and I can tell if I want to believe him or not." So if I look you in the eye and tell you I am going to run my car off a bridge, would you believe me? "No!" Why not? "Because I know you and you won't do something like that." Exactly! That is what God wants you to do with Him.

There are a few very simple ways to get to know God. One way is to read His word, the Bible. Another way is to pray to Him, which simply means to talk to Him as you would any one of your friends. Of course, you may question how or what is the proper way to address a most holy God. This reminded me of a story Jesus told about two men who went into the temple to pray.

Two men went up to the temple to pray, one a Pharisee and the other a tax collector. 11 The Pharisee stood up and prayed about himself: "God, I thank you that I am not like other men — robbers, evildoers, adulterers — or even like this tax collector. I fast twice a week and give a tenth of all I get." But the tax collector stood at a distance. He would not even look up to heaven, but beat his breast and said, "God, have mercy on me, a sinner." I tell you that this man, rather than the other, went home justified before God. For everyone who exalts himself will be humbled, and he who humbles

himself will be exalted. (Luke 18:10-14 NIV)

The very clear point is, come to God humbly and don't try to hide who you are because He already knows everything (omniscience). One of the clearest lessons that Jesus taught was that He didn't come to save those who were well or righteous but sinners, those who need a physician. So if we would just approach God honestly and openly, He will hear us. I often remember what I once heard, "God meets us where we are, but because He loves us so much, He refuses to leave us there." God proved that in my life and lifted me up out of the sin trap and the lies of Satan. He will do that for anyone who comes to Him and asks.

The bottom line of this chapter is: will you give God a chance to show up in your life, allowing Him the opportunity to do what He has promised to do for you?

Chapter Two

Let us press a little further into this awesome God of ours. We have a saying at the Cross Style Church, "Press into Jesus." We are so moved by His presence in our lives that it seems as though there is this big magnet inside of us that keeps pulling us into Him.

Jesus said that, "No one could come to Him unless the Father draws him." The thing that seems so amazing is that He is drawing us.

Now, don't think that God is only paying attention to the "super spiritual saints". Without God, we were drug addicts, alcoholics, sex addicts, prostitutes, and worshipers of the world however God has and continues to pay attention to us. Don't take my word for it, read the Scriptures.

> **On hearing this, Jesus said, "It is not the healthy who need a doctor, but the sick. But go and learn what this means: I desire mercy, not sacrifice. For I have not come to call the**

righteous, but sinners." (Matt 9:12-13 NIV)

Once again, that verse proves that God may have met you where you were, but He has no intention of leaving you there. That is His mercy.

Early in my walk with the Lord, He showed me His words in John chapter 15:16, "You didn't choose Me but I chose you." When I read those words and began to understand that God in the Person of Jesus Christ was revealing His plan to restore my life, I just had to know more.

I started to pray with an unrelenting prayer life. My goal was to seek the face of God. I read stories about how Jacob wrestled with God and man and prevailed.

So Jacob was left alone, and a man wrestled with him till daybreak. When the man saw that he could not overpower him, he touched the socket of Jacob's hip so that his hip was wrenched as he wrestled with the man. Then the man said, "Let me go, for it is daybreak." But Jacob replied, "I will not let you go unless you bless me." The man asked him, "What is your name?" "Jacob," he answered.

17

Then the man said, "Your name will no longer be Jacob, but Israel, because you have struggled with God and with men and have overcome." (Genesis 32:24-28 NIV)

I was amazed that the God I was told was angry and waiting to squash wicked people like me, was actually interactive, so tolerant, and truly interested in my request.

Armed with this new information, I attempted to stay up all night and pray to God to move in my life. Needless to say, tiredness prevailed and I was asleep in an hour. I awoke startled and felt like a failure and even a disappointment to God. I began to apologize and ask for forgiveness for being so weak. The funny thing was I didn't get smacked around for doing wrong; instead, I began to feel a new peace come over me.

Well, I had to investigate this peace. Looking up the word peace, I found:

Do not be anxious about anything, but in everything, by prayer and petition, with thanksgiving, present your requests to God. And the peace of God, which transcends all understanding, will guard your hearts and your minds

in Christ Jesus. (Philippians 4: 6-7 NIV)

I felt that God had rewarded me with peace just because I had made an attempt to "wrestle" with Him. Having learned that God knows every thought of man, and even the words that will come from his mouth before the man does, it was obvious that God knew I truly wanted to see Him. I was so encouraged that I continually went after Him, seeking and even meditating on the verses above. This truly was a breakthrough that I needed in my life!

I began to cry out to God. With tears and sobs, I began to exclaim, "Why didn't anyone tell me that I could have a personal and intimate relationship with You?" I truly asked this question every day in the same way for nearly two months then I heard, "That is what you are going to tell others." So here I am telling you, wherever you are, and no matter what condition you are in, God is seeking you for an intimate and personal relationship. Set aside your previous misconceptions about God and allow Him to reveal to you who He really is, God who is love!

The beginning of this relationship with God became even more personal. What I discovered was that the "outside God" had become the "inside God". Yet, I too was under the old way of thinking, that God was way up in heaven and I was left here on earth attempting to reach Him somehow. Guess what? You guessed it, I couldn't.

I tried to meditate on an image of what I thought heaven might look like and tried to visualize God sitting on His throne as I was standing in line behind others who also were looking to talk to Him. Think of a time you stood in line or camped overnight for your favorite concert ticket, hoping that they wouldn't be sold out before your turn, and you worried that you would go away dejected. How incredibly disappointed we would be if God treated us that way.

Fortunately, the Scriptures proved that I wasn't waiting in line.

> **Jesus replied, "If anyone loves me, he will obey my teaching. My Father will love him, and we will come to him and make our home with him." (John 14:23-24 NIV)**

What! Yeah, that's what I said, "what?" I simply asked, "You mean You came to me?" That was true because Jesus said, "No one can come to Me unless the Father draws them." So, the Father draws us through the Holy Spirit. The Spirit tugs, prods, woos, and pulls on us until we respond to Him. Even to our last breath, He continues to ask us to let Him in. This is known by many holiness movement believers as "prevenient" grace. This is the grace of God that goes before our salvation.

Armed with this new information, I was standing in awe of what God was saying. Simply that, He and Jesus, by way of Their Spirit, had already moved into me. Jesus doesn't just move into the neighborhood and stop by every once in a while. Nor does He just move into your house and take up your spare bedroom. He actually takes His rightful place inside your inner person. He created a place for Himself in man (humankind) that nothing else can fill.

Hence, the constant struggle in my former life and quite possibly your life was that we were always empty and tried desperately to fill with drugs, alcohol, sex, and many other things to no avail. The **"peace"** of God that surpasses all understanding can only come from Him and nothing else will ever be able to satisfy the need brought about by the empty space.

Then, God started to reveal something even more amazing; **Jesus is the focus**. I was starting to have revelation that it was God in the person of Jesus Christ that I was drawn to. The relationship God was starting with me wasn't with an invisible God, a God not seen, nor even a God that is not touchable, but rather a living, breathing, touchable person named Jesus.

> **That which was from the beginning, which we have heard, which we have seen with our eyes, which we have looked at and our hands have touched — this we proclaim concerning the Word of life. The life appeared; we have seen it and testify to it, and we proclaim to you the eternal life, which was with the Father and has appeared to us. We proclaim to you what we have seen and heard, so that you also may have fellowship with us. And our fellowship is with the Father and with his Son, Jesus Christ. (I John 1: 1-3 NIV)**

The Scriptures proved to me that it was Jesus Himself who wanted this relationship, and I really could believe Him. The working the Holy Spirit confirmed that I am a child of God.

I used to want to be anyone but me. I truly didn't know who I was or if I even liked me. Obviously, not a very fair approach, considering I didn't even attempt to get to know who I was. No problem for Jesus. He already knew of my dysfunctions and how to deal with them. Jesus isn't waiting for us to figure it all out and then come to Him all cleaned up and in our right mind. Seems to me, every demoniac in Scripture was destroyed and in need of repair when the Master approached them.

One story that talks about this is found in Mark chapter five. The demon possessed man was in terrible trouble considering that he was possessed by a "legion" of demons. When Jesus arrived on the scene this man had often times been chained by the villagers nearby to keep him from hurting anyone. Their attempts to bind him never worked, and he would continually terrify people to the point that they no longer wanted to go anywhere near him. What happened after the encounter with Jesus, we read in verse fifteen.

> **When they came to Jesus, they saw the man who had been possessed by the legion of demons, sitting there, dressed and in his right mind; and they were afraid. (Mark 5:15 NIV)**

It truly is an awesome thing to encounter God in person and be changed. It seems to bring out the astonishment by others, "Hey aren't you so and so the drunk, prostitute, druggie? What happened to you?" I met the Master Jesus Christ Himself and He changed me from the inside out. See, we seem to stay the same in physical appearance which seems to be what people judge us by. However, that is only the shell that carries around the real you.

God created us a body to move around in and to identify each other with, but that isn't who you are. The "who you are" inside is called a soul. This is also the part of you that will live on for all eternity along with your new body. Therefore, the question is not whether we live or die, but where we live out eternity. God's eternal purpose for His creation (you and I) is that we will live out eternity with Him.

> **The creation waits in eager expectation for the sons of God to be revealed. For the creation was subjected to frustration, not by its own choice, but by the will of the one who subjected it, in hope that the creation itself will be liberated from its bondage to decay and brought into the glorious freedom of the children of God.**

We know that the whole creation has been groaning as in the pains of childbirth right up to the present time. Not only so, but we ourselves, who have the first fruits of the Spirit, groan inwardly as we wait eagerly for our adoption as sons, the redemption of our bodies. For in this hope we were saved. But hope that is seen is no hope at all. Who hopes for what he already has? But if we hope for what we do not yet have, we wait for it patiently. (Romans 8:19-25 NIV)

We, as well as the earth, were created by God to have a relationship with Him. We also know from Scriptures that: "God desires all men to be saved and come to the knowledge of the truth" (1 Tim. 2:4). Therefore, having an intimate and personal relationship with Him is what He wants and what we have really been looking for in the things of the world. The things of the world will never suffice to fulfill all that we need to be complete and full beings. God Himself is the fulfillment of all things.

Chapter Three

If I was to title this chapter, it would be, **"The Emptiness of Religion."** Perhaps you already know what I am talking about. The congregations of the Christian church today are full of religious activity. They look good and mean well but have no substance to them. Recently, I was having lunch with Pastor Ray, a 70 year old retired Baptist preacher. He began to explain a meeting he had just come from with a dreaded look on his face. Pastor Ray why the long face? "I have just come from an hour and a half meeting with some church leaders and the whole discussion was, "What are we going to do about the deadness of the church today?"

Many congregations have programs, Bible studies, outreach ministries, and feed and clothe the "less fortunate" of their communities. However, they are no closer to Jesus than the lost. Jesus in His earthly ministry often spoke to the Pharisees (real God fearing and pious people) as hypocrites, snakes, and broods of vipers because they did all their activities out of self-righteousness. This is also the way many religious folks are today.

While at the Lazarus Center, in July of 2012, a woman came to us in need of food and a mattress to sleep on in a place she recently moved to. After settling her needs, I asked if she believed on the Lord Jesus Christ as her Lord and Savior. Her response was a resounding yes! So I then asked where she worshiped. I was not the least bit surprised at her response. She told me she used to worship at a certain Baptist church but was ostracized because of the clothing she wore. She stated that all she had to wear was shorts, and the ladies of the church gave her an ultimatum, "Either wear proper clothing or this isn't the place for you." She wanted to explain that she was poor and couldn't find other options right at that time but was too embarrassed to confess it. Here is how James wrote about that very action:

My brothers and sisters, as believers in our glorious Lord Jesus Christ, don't show favoritism. Suppose a man comes into your meeting wearing a gold ring and fine clothes, and a poor man in shabby clothes also comes in.

If you show special attention to the man wearing fine clothes and say, "Here's a good seat for you," but say to the poor man, "You stand there" or "Sit on the floor by my feet," have you not discriminated among yourselves and become judges with evil thoughts? Listen, my dear brothers: Has not God chosen those who are poor in the eyes of the world to be rich in faith and to inherit the kingdom He promised those who love him? But you have insulted the poor. (James 2: 1-6 NIV)

So you might be asking, what does this have to do with the question of, "Who am I to God...?" It is the fact that injurious actions by those who claim to be Christians keep the lost from seeking and finding. The poor, lost, confused, and bewildered simply walk away from Jesus because those who claim Christ are repelling instead of attracting. Please, if you are struggling to see Jesus in religion, get away fast and seek Jesus for who He is. I assure you, He won't let you down.

I truly believe one of the most confusing things I experienced growing up and just didn't know any different was that, I thought I had to find Jesus in a building, or in religious activities, or in my own cleaned up efforts; what a mess! This led me to believe that I certainly could never join the "Christian Club" since according to my grandma and mom; I was only a filthy little boy and would never amount to anything. Now hold that up against the religious, well dressed people and - *whoa you're out man! Give it up; there is no hope for you.*

Next came the day of my own prosperity in the form of money, influence, power, and all around nice guy...on the outside. So you know what I did with that? I got married to a religious girl and went to church in order to please her. Since I thought God hung out in the church building, I figured I could show up and prove my grandma and mom wrong after all these years. I could now show them that I had met God.

So how do you think that went for me? If you answered, "Terribly wrong," you answered correctly. Not only that, I got mad at God for the hypocrisy of those in the church building, as if it was somehow His fault. I am so relieved to tell you, it wasn't His fault. That nice girl and I got a very non-emotional divorce.

I then reached out to the pastor of the church only to be told that it must somehow have been my fault and there just wasn't anything he could do to help me. Oh, just so you know, on the inside of all that was "religious hierarchy." Her daddy was a pillar of the church, and well, no one wanted to help me, the outsider. Praise be to God that He accepts the outsiders and loves them the same as the insiders.

So did this change how God felt about me? I assure you for a few months afterward, I asked myself that very question. I wondered, since I wasn't in the church any more, if God was with me. I had approached my whole relationship with God (if that is what you want to call it) on my ability to stay cleaned up, think right, act right, do right, and most certainly worship right. I found myself lashing out, acting out, and most certainly thinking badly. So, I walked away and went right back to living "my" life on "my" terms, only to find out years later, that is what I had been doing in my three year "church building" relationship with God. I was living in a "relationship" with God on my terms.

My relationship with God wasn't based on what God wanted, although, I was told it was. I believed God was up in Heaven giving us a list of things to do like the "Ten Commandments." I thought we were just to live out a good life and God would let us in Heaven when life is all over. Are you confused, or can you relate this in your life? Don't feel bad, many do.

To carry this one step further, I walked away from more than the church building; I walked away from God. As time went by, my life turned worse, meaning, I began to act out more of my hate on other relationships I had with people. I married several more times, leaving a wake of destruction in my path.

I began and then continued to increase my drinking and party life-style. I simply didn't care about anyone, including myself. Confusion as to who I was became a norm in my life. Most of the time, I didn't want to know who I was, and I would constantly search for my identity in other people or my careers.

During a few really low spots of my life, I had guilty feelings over my choices and would go to church somewhere and put a lot of money in the plate thinking somehow God surely would like that and maybe He would let me back in. Of course, this never did bring about the results I wanted. The key word in this sentence is "I." No matter what you try to do or how many times you do it, you cannot meet

God on your terms. A humbled and broken heart is what God wants. I didn't know that, since to me, it was all about how we conducted our own lives.

I am so relieved to be telling you today, it isn't about what we do or don't do or how well we do it. It is all about God who is Love, and that Love is an overwhelming force of hope, assurance, and a drastic need in all of our lives.

I continually find myself in awe of God for who He is and the immeasurable greatness of His love toward all of us. The more I seek Him the more He reveals, and this is true of anyone who comes to Him. The mystery that so many "religious" people cloud Jesus in is their lack of seeking, therefore, their lack of finding.

So I have realized the, "Who I am to God..." isn't about who I neither am to the religious orders of today nor would have been at any time in history. Jesus never taught religion, only relationship. He never lived out a religious lifestyle for us to follow. He lived out of a relationship with God lifestyle. Jesus is all about a personal and intimate relationship with each person, and that is where true peace and security is found.

This personal relationship is done through reconciliation with God through the Person Jesus

Christ His son. In the Bible, the apostle Paul explains it this way:

> So from now on we regard no one from a worldly point of view. Though we once regarded Christ in this way, we do so no longer. Therefore, if anyone is in Christ, he is a new creation; the old has gone, the new has come! All this is from God, who reconciled us to himself through Christ and gave us the ministry of reconciliation: that God was reconciling the world to himself in Christ, not counting man's sins against them. And he has committed to us the message of reconciliation. We are therefore Christ's ambassadors, as though God were making his appeal through us. We implore you on Christ's behalf: Be reconciled to God. God made him who had no sin to be sin for us, so that in him we might become the righteousness of God. (2 Corinthians 5: 16-21 NIV)

The apostle John wrote about this relationship in many ways throughout his Gospel. I chose this one because of the fact that God wants a "Father to child" relationship.

Yet to all who received Him, to those who believed in His name, He gave the right to become children of God— children born not of natural descent, nor of human decision or a husband's will, but born of God. (John 1: 12-13 NIV)

The significance of this verse is so overwhelming that we must pause and take it in. By accepting Christ's work on the cross of Calvary and believing that it was done to destroy Satan's hold on our lives, we become children of God.

I no longer, nor do you; have to look to your earthly parents as the reason for your existence. We are born of God through Christ's resurrection from the dead. This truth gave me a whole new sense of purpose and quality of life. I now experience every day a freedom of living that can only be expressed by the indwelling Christ and the peace that surpasses all understanding.

If you are struggling with, "Who am I, and how can I have peace in my life?" just call on Jesus, and He will answer you before you even finish the question.

Turning again to the Scriptures, Jesus is teaching the crowds about how the generation of that day wasn't accepting Him as the Messiah, who they had longed for and had been praying to come for centuries:

> **At that time Jesus said, "I praise you, Father, Lord of heaven and earth, because you have hidden these things from the wise and learned, and revealed them to little children. Yes, Father, for this was your good pleasure.**
>
> **"All things have been committed to me by my Father. No one knows the Son except the Father, and no one knows the Father except the Son and those to whom the Son chooses to reveal him.**
>
> **"Come to me, all you who are weary and burdened, and I will give you rest. Take my yoke upon you and learn from me, for I am gentle and humble in heart, and you will find rest for your souls. For my yoke is easy and my burden is light." (Matt 11: 25-30 NIV)**

"Come to Me," is a fascinating study in the original language of the New Testament. The word "come" is an invitation, not a command. Then it is followed by "to" (pros) in Greek and means "turn toward" something or someone. Here Jesus uses it to say, "Turn towards Me". The amazing picture that comes out of the two words is that the very moment you turn your heart (that is your inner thoughts) toward Jesus, He is all over you and you run right into Him.

Just glance His way, for He is standing right there with arms wide open to grab a hold of you and hug you like you have never ever been hugged before.

The truth revealed is that we cannot find God in the, **"deadness of religion."** We only find Him in an open, honest, and intimate relationship as He pours out Himself into us. We are not saved by works but by grace. A simple way of understanding is a statement Dr. Manley often says, "God loves you and there is nothing you can do about it. He has made up His mind and nothing you can do will change that. He loves you - just accept it."

I am praying for you as you continue reading to find the relationship Jesus wants with you simply because He has chosen you to have this intimacy with. It isn't based on how well you do "religion."

Chapter Four

Chapter four is a result of a sermon I preached in September of 2012. I thought it was appropriate to share with you in this transformation of life that comes from knowing the person of Jesus Christ.

It was early on in my relationship with the Lord that I began to realize I wasn't afraid of life as I once was. I have learned to turn my fears over to Jesus who is the master of all situations.

It isn't that fears don't come up, because they certainly do, but it is in the way we react to them that determines the outcome. As you read through the sermon, find for yourself both the truth that is in the Scriptures and the assurance that Jesus is in fact in control.

The Thing You Fear, Fears Him.

We are going to take a short journey with Jesus and His disciples. Our journey begins one evening in the late summer of AD 28. Earlier that day, Jesus was teaching many things concerning the Kingdom of God in a town called Capernaum.

Capernaum is a seaside town on the northwest shore of the Sea of Galilee. Capernaum was a busy port town, full of a diversity of cultures, and a town where Jesus spent a lot of His ministry time. This particular day Jesus taught the crowd about "planting seeds," "growing seeds," and the "mustard seed" which were all parables used to describe the Word of God and the Kingdom of God and how it grows by His words.

Jesus left Capernaum and headed toward the shore, but He wasn't alone. In town were the original 12 disciples and a multitude of town folk and curious travelers. Jesus' intentions were to take a short sail across the Sea of Galilee to a town called Gergesa about 5 miles away to the east.

The delay came from the many questions the crowd was shouting. Jesus took time to stop and answer their questions, but the crowd was so thick and compressing in around Him that He had to board the boat. Being pushed a little bit away from the shore, He began to speak to them again. As the sun was beginning to set, Jesus said to His disciples, "Let us go over to the other side. With that our journey begins.

That day when evening came, He said to his disciples, "Let us go over to the other side." Leaving the crowd behind, they took Him along, just as He was, in

38

the boat. There were also other boats with Him. A furious squall came up, and the waves broke over the boat, so that it was nearly swamped. Jesus was in the stern, sleeping on a cushion. The disciples woke Him and said to Him, "Teacher, don't you care if we drown?" He got up, rebuked the wind and said to the waves, "Quiet! Be still!" Then the wind died down and it was completely calm.

He said to his disciples, "Why are you so afraid? Do you still have no faith?"

They were terrified and asked each other, "Who is this? Even the wind and the waves obey Him!" (Mark 4: 35-41 NIV)

Four points:
1) The Direction v. 35
2) The Destroyer v. 37
3) The Directive v. 39
4) The Doubt and its twin (fear) v. 40 & 41

Point 1) The Direction: Jesus said to his disciples, "Let us go over to the other side."

For many of us, as we began our journey with Jesus, every step seemed to be silver-lined. We went along without a care in the world as we trotted past fields of beautiful flowers basking in the sun. Many of us said, "Oh, this is the life," peace and tranquility just seemed to be an everyday experience.

Some of you might have been just like the disciples, listening very carefully to every word Jesus spoke. Some of you got to see miracle after miracle as you have journeyed along with Jesus from town to town. If the truth be known, it is as though you never suffered an attack from the enemy. You might even think you were living in a supernatural bubble.

Your career as a disciple of Christ looks promising. It is as though you are learning from the Master Himself, front row seats in the classroom of God. You are getting hands on training for your new vocation. In fact, it won't be too long and you will be sent out to do some of the same miracles that Jesus has been doing.

Pretty impressive isn't it?

Some of you are like Peter. Bold, confident, proud of your physical strength and abilities. You are ready to defend Christ at any cost, even if that means pulling out your switchblade and cutting off a man's ear.

Then there are some of you who are like Matthew. You're smart, quick of mind, real wizards in the financial world; you rely on your intelligence to get you by.

I can't leave out those of you who are like John, gentle, kind, peacekeepers, and everyone's friend.

Yep!!!

Jesus gave a directive, and we are off and sailing. **What a thrill! What a life!**

As we leave the shore of Capernaum, the sun is setting behind us, and we can feel the heat warming our backs. The sea is calm, which is typical for that time of day, and a light breeze begins to cool our faces as we all look forward to the journey that lies ahead.

While we settle in the boat, rowing out just far enough to hoist a sail, Jesus says (paraphrased), "It's been a long day boys; I'm going to get some rest. This cushion looks really comfortable; wake Me when we get to the other side."

"Sure thing Jesus!" proclaims Peter in his very confident and strong voice. Peter might have been thinking, *I know what I'm doing. I've sailed this sea a thousand times before. Why I know every ripple it makes. We will get you to the other side...no problem!*

With that Peter begins to bark out his instructions. "Row those oars; hoist that sail. You heard Jesus. We have got to get to the other side." Jesus turns away with a slight smile, a gentle nod of His head, lies down, and quickly falls asleep.

*** Have you ever gotten your assignment from Jesus? You know, the **direction** you were "supposed" to go?
*** Did you set out with great confidence and expectation?

How quickly we begin to rely on ourselves to pull off the work of the Lord. We feel strong and capable. We even go so far as to convince ourselves that nothing will stop us. We have this under control!

Point 2) The Destroyer:

What happens is that the "Destroyer" has every intention to destroy you. He not only wants to destroy the plan but you along with the plan. He (meaning Satan) will stop at nothing to accomplish that very thing. We see that right here in these passages:

> **A furious squall came up, and the waves broke over the boat, so that it was nearly swamped. (Mark 4:37 NIV)**

Then all of a sudden out of absolutely nowhere, a ferocious mind boggling storm of life knocks you to the ground! Your very core is rocked!

Despair overtakes your joy; fear steals your faith; clouds obscure your hope; and terror overcomes your assurance! What do you do when the very struggle for your life is upon you? Who do you turn to? Who then is your resource of help? The disciples were wondering the same thing at this very moment.

The disciples have come under attack. What appeared to be a simple journey over to the other side, a journey not unlike many others they have taken before, has just become their single greatest living nightmare.

The Destroyer has shown up!

The Bible tells us a fierce windstorm arose. A sudden and violent windstorm known as a squall has begun to throw their little boat around like a little toy boat in a bathtub with a three year old. The men are tossed around like rag dolls. The waves are spilling gallons of water into the boat with each crashing blow.

The Sea of Galilee can be seen as an example of how our lives can be. What appears to be quiet and peaceful at one moment, can suddenly become terrorizing and out of control the next.

Let me share a little more background about the Sea of Galilee. She is fed by the Jordan River coming down from the north. It is 13 miles long and eight miles wide at its widest point. Its surface is 730 feet below that of the Mediterranean Sea and is 150 feet deep at its deepest point. Its shape is like a pear with its narrow end pointing southward. Like the Dead Sea, it is set deep among hills which rise on its east side to a height of about 2,000 feet.

The reason for the sudden and violent storm is caused by a valley through these mountains. As the hot air of the desert to the east side of the mountains gathers strength, it will be forced through this narrow valley and become streamlined and powerful. As the hot air hits the surface of the cool Galilee water, a storm is almost instantly formed and releases its power, causing 20 foot swells in the sea. The storms are sudden, without warning, and are very violent.

So we see the **Destroyer** come on the scene in order to stop the mission that Jesus and the disciples are on. The destroyer will try to do the same thing to us as we continue to be directed by Jesus in this life.

The disciples are attempting to grab a hold of anything solid as they are gasping for air between the crashing blows of the sea. In our own lives, we find ourselves attempting to find something solid to hang onto when struggles knock us off our feet. We keep grasping for things visible, perhaps something physical we used in our past when problems came at us. Not unlike before, they just don't seem to work.

***Why is that?

 *** Why doesn't that make us feel secure?

What we cling to in the physical has no power to stop the storm. It just isn't capable of dealing with the struggle. It just can't get to the heart of the problem.

Finally, someone remembered who was in the boat with them. They went to Jesus (who by the way was sleeping rather comfortably during all this) and shouted, **"Jesus, Jesus wake up!! Don't you care that we are about to die???"**

It would prove out rather quickly that they didn't know Jesus had power over nature. They were shocked that Jesus didn't seem the least bit concerned about dying in the sea that day.

Listen to what they say next:

> **"Teacher, don't you care if we drown?" (Mark 4:38)**

Don't you care if **we**...they included Jesus in that **"we"**.

I can almost imagine Jesus' face as He stood up and brushed aside His soaking wet hair - A look of disappointment perhaps, but first things first.

*** The 3rd point is the Directive.

**He got up, rebuked the wind and said
to the waves, "Quiet! Be still!" Then
the wind died down and it was
completely calm. (Mark 4:39 NIV)**

Jesus rebuked the wind. The word **"rebuked" in
v. 39** is the same word Jesus used when dealing with
the demons.

When Jesus breaks the power of the unclean
spirit, which is the representative of evil powers, the
sovereignty of God begins to make its way through
His words.

When Jesus acts in this way, He demonstrates that
He stands entirely on the side of God, and the power
of God is His. He simply takes control of the situation
by the very words He speaks. Therefore, shear
power is then released into the situations of our
lives. Nothing is outside of His control which is very
evident in the Scriptures we are studying.

Listen again to verse 39:

**He got up, rebuked the wind and said
to the waves, "Quiet! Be still!" Then
the wind died down and it was
completely calm. (Mark 4:39 NIV)**

The word in the Greek for quiet is **siopao:** which
means

Peace — Cease thy tossing: **Be still** — Cease thy roaring; literally, be quiet!

For the first time, in just over a year that the disciples have been with Jesus, they see firsthand that He also has mastery over nature.

Sure, they saw hundreds of healings, demons fleeing, and lives changed, but this, this shocked them. This was a hard thing to wrap their minds around.

Remember some of these men were experienced fishermen on this sea. They knew deep down that this storm was unlike any they had ever experienced before, for two reasons. First, this storm was occurring at night and storms were not common at night but rather very rare. Most storms would happen in the early afternoon hours and they wouldn't go out fishing then. Fishing was always better at night anyway. Second, they were about 2.5 miles into this 5 mile trip which was farther than they would normally travel to fish anyway. Add it all up, and they were sure they were going to die!

Have you ever been in a struggle like this?

Has life become hopeless?

Perhaps you even thought you were going to die?

Maybe you just wanted to die!

Have you ever felt like you just couldn't catch your breath because of life's pressures?

Have you ever just wondered where to find the strength to take another step?

You're not alone. The disciples that hung out with Jesus every day were experiencing those very questions at this moment.

What we see here is that Jesus is bigger than the storm. Jesus is the solution to all of life's struggles. Jesus is the solution to your life.

Jesus told us that we would have struggles in this world, but that we are to be courageous for He has conquered the world (John 16:33).

Point #4) **The Doubt and its twin (fear) Vs 40,41**

> **He said to his disciples, "Why are you so afraid? Do you still have no faith?"**

They were terrified and asked each other, "Who is this? Even the wind and the waves obey him!" (Mark 4:40-41 NIV)

Jesus wasn't just asking a simple question or making a passing remark. After He commanded that nature get in line and settle down, He asked a stern question about their fear.

He uses the Greek word **deilos** which is an adjective and the subject of the sentence, so all focus is on the word **afraid**. This word is only used 3 times in the New Testament.

Twice the word is used in the account of this story, once in Matthew 8:2, here in Mark 4:40, and also in Revelation 21:8 which reads:

But the cowardly, the unbelieving, the vile, the murderers, the sexually immoral, those who practice magic arts, the idolaters and all liars — their place will be in the fiery lake of burning sulfur. This is the second death. (Revelation 21:8 NIV)

The word for cowardly in Rev. 21:8 is our word **deilos:** To fear, be timid, speaking of Christians who through cowardice give way under persecutions and apostatize. Meaning, they turn away from the grace of God.

Doubt in the person of Jesus will bring fear and utter loss of life.

*** We must learn something from all this, and that is, our assurance is in Jesus. We are to fix our sight on Him and His plan. We are to be submitted to His direction.

*** "The wind ceased and there was a great calm"

When we fix our sight on Jesus, we receive a supernatural calm and a peace that exceeds comprehension.

Satan has but one purpose - to destroy you and me, the ones created in the very image of God. Satan wants to cause fear, restlessness, and struggles. But remember this as children of God, we no longer operate in the bondage of fear or our past. Jesus liberated us with His finished work on the Cross of Calvary.

Ours is an assurance of the victory that Jesus has already won. It isn't a victory that we have to go out and struggle through to win or even attempt to accomplish. It is a victory we only need to believe in and accept. This then brings rest.

"As you live out your life in Christ you can truly feel that you are filled with power and dominion. Your emptiness is filled with peace and contentment. Your jealousy and hatred is replaced with understanding. Your most paralyzing fears can be met with courage. Your need to please vanishes, and in its place appears a wonderful freedom to be your unique self." (Healed Without Scares Bishop David Evans)

There was a purpose for that storm that early evening on the Sea of Galilee, and there are purposes for the struggles you and I face as well.

"See the greater grace is not deliverance but preservation. God wants to deliver you in the midst of your trial, before He moves you out of it." (Healed Without Scares Bishop David Evans)

If Jesus would have stopped that storm before they started to cross the sea, what lesson would have been taught? What lesson would have been learned? If God never allowed us to go through some struggles, how would we learn to go to Him? The greatest lessons you will ever learn will not come by avoiding the test but taking the test.

"Our true deliverance is that we are changed in the midst of our trials before the trial is changed."

What the disciples learned that day, from what seemed like absolute loss of life, would carry them through the rest of their lives because their focus was changed from self-sourced to God-sourced. It was through the struggle they learned dependence upon and assurance in Jesus.

Now I want to take you back for just a moment to verse 35. I want you to learn something that the disciples missed.

The verse reads:

That day when evening came, he said to his disciples, "Let us go over to the other side." (Mark 4:35 NIV)

Jesus had received His travel plans from God the Father and He was able to sleep during this ferocious storm because He knew without doubt that He and those with Him were going to the other side no matter what Satan threw at them. See, failure wasn't an option. Failure is never an option when God declares something.

So Jesus asked the question, "Why are you so afraid? Do you still have no faith?"

The disciples looked at the storm and not the solution. **Doubt has a twin and it is fear!**

Even today, people doubt that there is a God who really loves and expresses His love for them. In just a few years from this scene, the fulfillment of God's love would be Jesus laying down His life on the Cross of Calvary to atone for the sins of all of mankind.

We, as born again children of God, are called to live above fear and doubt. Ours is a freedom to live in complete rest in Jesus.

So what is our assurance today? Simply this: **Jesus is risen!** He conquered death, sin, self, and has overcome the world.

He stands with His arms wide open and pleads, "**COME ...TO... ME!!!!**"

As you can see, the destroyer is nothing more than a bunch of hot air that comes in to upset the balance or calmness that Jesus is. If you seek Jesus, become submissive to Him, and continually focus on Him, then the storms of your life will calm down.

Chapter Five

Again, I am using a sermon I preached in September of 2012, to express a deep and personal truth Jesus has brought me through. I was seven and Marla was four. She would have turned five in April of 1972, had she not died in my arms on Saturday, January 7, 1972.

Marla was my sister and best friend. I totally had the best of intentions of protecting her from anything and everything. We were abandoned by our mom on two separate occasions which led to our dad divorcing her. After that, our paternal grandfather convinced our dad to give us up and turn us over to foster care. He did just that.

Marla and I spent two years in state foster care and bounced around to three different homes. I was so grateful that we weren't separated. At some point in 1970, my dad was able to bring us home. A few years later, Marla died. I lost it and went into a state of shock. I became catatonic for several months and simply blacked out. I did not remember anything for the next year or so.

I will admit, I had spent a lot of time in my early walk with Jesus searching out a reason for all this junk in our lives. Marla and I were sexually abused. I also suffered much beatings and psychological abuse. But Marla's death was what broke me. I am no longer searching for a reason since I know the truth. Satan is the one who causes all sorts of evil destructive things. God is the restorer of those things to those who trust and have a personal intimate relationship with Him.

I have also learned that everything in the Kingdom of God seems to be backward from the things of the world. I, like most men, had found my comfort in the things I could accomplish. Since I was very successful in the sales profession, I competed for the top management positions that offered the best income and "risk reward". I even pressed my life to the edge of no reason in order to own and run my own corporation where no one could rule me. I truly believed in my heart that if I accomplished that, I would have peace and happiness and everything would be okay. Oh, how wrong I was! I later found peace and joy in losing it all and no longer depending on myself to accomplish anything but counting on Jesus to accomplish His plans.

That's why I found a lot of hope in these verses and many like them throughout Isaiah. In God's view, our accomplishments mean absolutely nothing compared to His accomplishments, and our goals are sub-par to His.

> **"For my thoughts are not your thoughts, neither are your ways my ways," declares the LORD. "As the heavens are higher than the earth, so are my ways higher than your ways and my thoughts than your thoughts." (Isaiah 55: 8-9 NIV)**

Walk through this sermon with me and see how the losing all the physical stuff is of no real consequence to the eternal blessing in Jesus.

The Goodness of God

And we know that all things work together for good to those who love God, to those who are the called according to *His* purpose. (Romans 8:28 NKJV)

That verse of the Bible has become the "claim all" of every unexplainable tragedy in a Christian's life. But I must ask the question, does that make the pain go away? Does that in some magical way console the depth of despair a parent experiences when one of their children die? Or does it really answer the question of "why" do tragedies happen? I would have to admit I have no answer to any of those questions.

One of the most asked questions by Christians and non-Christians alike is, "Why do tragedies happen?" Is it a fair question? Does it deserve any of our time? I think it deserves a proper answer. My answer would be to take our focus off the tragedy and focus on Jesus.

Those who are in a relationship with Jesus have an "attitude" that super-exceeds that of those who are merely religious or those who do not know Jesus at all. I know a Christian family who tragically lost their four year old daughter in the driveway of their family home when their seventeen year old son pulled out and did not see her in time to avoid striking her. I know personally what it is like to have my sister, who was my best friend, die in my arms when she was only four and I seven years old. I know what it is like to mourn with a nation who has been attacked by terrorist causing thousands to die senselessly.

Today I want to share with you a story of a man who lost everything, a man who like any other, grieved and mourned at the very depth of his soul. I want to share with you a man who had an intimate and very powerful relationship with God before, during, and after the tragedies. That man's name is Job.

Job, as we know, went through some of the most heart wrenching tragedies conceivable. Job suffered the kind of tragedies that would rip the very heart out of the strongest of people. Job was attacked from every side by Satan per God's okay.

Satan destroyed Job's land, cattle, and other livestock. Satan destroyed the lives of Job's servants, and then he destroyed his children. You would think that Job, or anyone for that matter, when faced with these tragedies, would be overwhelmed, grieved, and then angry, and as some would do, get mad at God. I won't take away the fact that Job grieved and mourned. We certainly know he asked God "why." But the point that comes out of this is Job's "attitude".

Lately, Jesus has been pressing me with the word "attitude". The simple definition is, "a state of mind or feeling." What I have been able to discover is that my attitude has a direct affect on my reaction to the things that happen in my life. If my attitude is, "I don't care," then whatever it is I don't care about, has very little affect on my daily life. If it is something I care about deeply, then my reaction to anything that tries to take that away from me will be profound and can lead to further complications. To test this theory, give a five year old some candy then try to take it back. You will be in for a fight.

As Jesus walked me through the first two chapters of Job, I was given a firsthand account of a man whose attitude and focus was on that of God and not the tragedies that wiped out everything he had.

Point one: Our Attitude Determines Our Reaction.

Job did not blame God, nor get mad at God, nor turn away from his relationship with God. In fact, listen to what Job said:

He said, "Naked I came from my mother's womb, And naked I shall return there. The Lord gave and the Lord has taken away. Blessed be the name of the Lord."
Through all this Job did not sin nor did he blame God. (Job 1:21-22 NASB)

Job didn't blame God; Job blessed God. **How** is that even possible? Can you really even grasp that kind of attitude? How can that be? Was Job speaking in a delirious frame of mind? **Not at all** - Job was in love with God.

Job's relationship with God was one of the deepest kinds of love. It was the kind of love that super-exceeds possessions and life itself! Job's relationship with God was fixed on God and in God. His attitude was, "God is God, and I can accept anything He wants." Job refused to allow anything to come between him and God.

Now, you might be thinking, *how could this be?* The answer is that Job found his strength in the

Lord. We even sing, "The joy of the Lord is my strength." Do you believe that?

See, Job didn't try to understand or deal with all this by his own understanding or intellect. Job was an elder and wise man who all the people around him came for advice and knowledge. But that wasn't what Job wanted to rely on to get him through this mess. Job didn't allow feelings and emotions to determine his reaction and somehow disgrace God in the process of some tirade.

Job knew God intimately and interacted continually with God, therefore, on the day of intense tragedy, Job was not led away. Job knew that God was in control and that He would see him through.

But hey, that isn't where the story ends. Satan had done his damage and went back to roaming around the earth looking for another victim. He was like a tornado that just ripped through your neighborhood and moved on to the next one.

Job was left in the wake of tragedy, yet he didn't look at himself. Because of Job's oneness with God, he didn't make this about himself. Job went about the consoling of his wife and that of the servants' families. Of course, the clean-up of this mess had to be done.

So as Job was busy about all that, something else was taking place in the heavenly realms.

Again there was a day when the sons of God came to present themselves before the Lord, and Satan also came among them to present himself before the Lord. The Lord said to Satan, "Where have you come from?" Then Satan answered the Lord and said, "From roaming about on the earth and walking around on it." (Job 2:1-2 NASB)

I don't know about you, but after reading chapter one, I had to stop to catch my breath. I mean, it was very overwhelming to consider all that had taken place. I really was pressed to consider my attitude about it all.

And now there is another conversation between God and Satan. What does God say?

The Lord said to Satan, "Have you considered My servant Job?" (Job 2:3 NASB)

God, for the second time, used the word "considered" which in Hebrew is (soom; siym), and it has many uses. One of which is the, **"taking something into ones grasp or putting hands on to arrest."** So a literal meaning could be, "Have you considered putting your hands on My servant?" This is exactly what happens.

But before we get to that part of the story, I want to point out to you what God has to say about Job:

> **The Lord said to Satan, "Have you considered My servant Job? For there is no one like him on the earth, a blameless and upright man fearing God and turning away from evil. And he still holds fast his integrity, although you incited Me against him to ruin him without cause." (Job 2:3 NASB)**

God praised Job! Right in the face of the enemy, God honored Job, a man, declaring him blameless and upright! How would you like God to declare before the enemy that you are blameless and upright?

God was honored by Job's suffering just as He was by Jesus' suffering on the cross of Calvary. We know that Jesus suffered like no one has ever suffered before or since.

As our story continues in chapter two, Satan has become very angry. He was angry because God was glorified and pleased with Job. There was no egg on God's face because of a negative reaction by Job.

I have to ask, do you see the relationship between God and this man named Job? Do you see a love that is unbreakable and immoveable? Job didn't love God for what God could do for him. It wasn't a relationship built on favors, or you bless me, and I'll praise you and tell all my buddies about you. It wasn't like that. This was a relationship built on unconditional love and focused on the person of God and not the gifts of God.

I have learned this about God's love; I learned it from Dr. Manley. As humans, we fall in love because we need something. So we fall in love with our spouse, as an example. Why, because there is a need in our life which that person can fulfill, such as companionship, help in the times of need, etc., but that is not how it is with God.

God, who is love, created us because He loves. God doesn't love us because He needs something from us. God is all sufficient and doesn't need anything because He lacks nothing. The fact is He loved us, therefore, He needs us. God's love comes from His nature which is sinless, and before we are transformed by God, our love comes from a nature of sinfulness. I will love you as long as you meet a need or two in my life. But hey, the minute you refuse to meet my need, see ya, I don't love you anymore.

Job's experience proves to me that the love of God can be lived out in a human being. My love for God, or anyone for that matter, does not need to be based on what they can or cannot do for me. Instead, love can be based on, "What can I do for you" or "How can I meet the needs of your life."

It is when we come to the knowledge of God's love and rest in the assurance that He is in control, that we can have peace in the middle of tragedies. Job looked beyond the physical and rested in his spiritual relationship with God. You might even say Job knew something about Paul's Letter to the Ephesians in the sixth chapter which teaches that we don't fight with flesh and blood but against spiritual darkness.

What was Satan's reaction to Job's attitude? Anger! Satan was spitting mad and fired back at God:

Satan answered the Lord and said, "Skin for skin! Yes, all that a man has he will give for his life. However, put forth Your hand now, and touch his bone and his flesh; he will curse You to Your face." (Job 2:4-5 NASB)

Satan was spitting mad that Job didn't get mad at God and turn away in defiance.

Hey, if you want to get under the skin of Satan, if you want to hit a nerve, then praise God in your storm! Glorify God in your tragedies! Shout hallelujah in the face of danger!

Do you see what is happening here? Satan isn't in control of this. He has to have permission from God. God is sovereign, and He says how far it can go.

In chapter two, verse seven, Satan infects Job with boils from the bottom of his feet to the top of his head. Satan was convinced this would break this man of God. He stood back wringing his hands and snarling, "I got him now!"

To make matters worse, as Job sat in the pile of ashes scraping the boils, his wife approaches. Oh, this excited Satan because he could see the look on her face and the disgust in her heart. See, it wasn't only Job's children that died; they were hers also!

Job's wife was confused, overwhelmed, and angry. She wasn't coming to Job to comfort him. Listen to what she says;

Then his wife said to him, "Do you still hold fast your integrity? Curse God and die!" (Job 2:9 NASB)

Now the last person any of us would expect to challenge our relationship with God would be our spouse. Yet at the very worst moment anyone of us could fathom going through, that is exactly what Job faced. But Job knew that God was closer to him than even his closest friend. His relationship with God remained his focus, and his attitude was that, "God is in control and He loves me."

Even though these horrific and incomprehensible events took place, "The love of God that surpasses knowledge," remained Job's focus; it remained his hope.

Job wouldn't allow his own wife to distract him from his relationship with God, nor to knock him off focus, nor change his attitude. Listen to Job's reply;

But he said to her, "You speak as one of the foolish women speaks. Shall we indeed accept good from God and not accept adversity?" In all this, Job did not sin with his lips. (Job 2:10 NASB)

So why is it that we have the story of Job in our Bible?

Be of sober *spirit,* be on the alert. Your adversary, the devil, prowls around like a roaring lion, seeking someone to devour. (I Peter 5:8 NASB)

The battle still rages! The enemy of God and your soul is still in the business of getting you to fall!

But more importantly, God wants us to know that He passionately wants oneness with us. It was in this oneness between God and Job that Job could glorify God in spite of the physical circumstances. Job knew God intimately and experienced Him in his everyday life. Furthermore, Job knew that even if he died, he would see God face to face. Job rested in the unbreakable Love of God.

The reason Job didn't sin during all this wasn't because he was a religious person and white knuckled his way through it. He got through it because he was and still is, in love with God for who He is.

Do you have this oneness with Jesus today?

Are you resting in an unbreakable relationship with Him?

Are you in love with Jesus?

Your relationship with God isn't about good and bad, right or wrong, a laundry list of rules you've got to keep. It is all about His love. Love is relational and Jesus is relational, therefore, He is calling us into a love relationship with Himself. A relationship that will prove to be more than you could ever experience without Him.

As a result of this kind of love relationship that God Himself wants with each person, we can all experience a worry free life. If you want to beat anxiety without drugs, nervousness without alcohol, dread without living in some fantasy land, and check out of reality, then get into Jesus quickly! Turn your hopes and dreams over to the One who can do all things and where failure is not an option.

Another sermon I would like to share with you came from my very own personal experience. I hope you enjoy learning about a peace that surpasses all we can comprehend.

The Worry Free Christian

Be anxious for nothing, but in everything by prayer and supplication, with thanksgiving, let your requests be made known to God; and the peace of God, which surpasses all understanding, will guard your hearts and minds through Christ Jesus. (Phil 4:6-8 NKJV)

Point I. **Stress less**

The word Paul chose to use is "anxious." In the Greek, it is "merimnao" which means to worry, to concern yourself with..., too have your thoughts occupied with, or meditating on.

We as Christians are not to have our time consumed by worry and anxiety over the needs of our lives. In fact, Jesus tells us in Matthew 6:25:

Therefore I say to you, do not worry about your life, what you will eat or what you will drink, nor about your body, what you will put on. Is not life

more than food and the body more than clothing? (Matthew 6:25 NKJV)

As you can see, Jesus went to the central nervous system of all human worry which is the concerns about everyday living. In fact, it is the concerns of everyday living that causes the majority of health problems people suffer from today.

The major focus of what Paul is saying in Philippians 4:6 is no matter what you are in need of, there is nothing too small or too large for God to be concerned about or unable to accomplish in your life.

Point: II. **Supplicating**

The word supplication is the Greek word **"deesis" and simply means to make a request.** It can also mean to beg.

We are to come to God with an absolute assurance that we have a right to be in His presence and simply ask Him whatever it is we feel we need to ask. There are simply hundreds of statements in the Bible that verify what I just said. Here are a few of my favorites:

So Jesus answered and said to them, "Have faith in God. For assuredly, I say to you, whoever says to this mountain,

Be removed and be cast into the sea, and does not doubt in his heart, but believes that those things he says will be done, he will have whatever he says. Therefore I say to you, whatever things you ask when you pray, believe that you receive *them,* and you will have *them."* (Mark 11:22-24 NKJV)

Most assuredly, I say to you, he who believes in Me, the works that I do he will do also; and greater *works* than these he will do, because I go to My Father. And whatever you ask in My name, that I will do, that the Father may be glorified in the Son. If you ask anything in My name, I will do *it.* (John 14:12-14 NKJV)

If you abide in Me, and My words abide in you, you will ask what you desire, and it shall be done for you. (John 15:7 NKJV)

Let us therefore come boldly to the throne of grace, that we may obtain

mercy and find grace to help in time of need. (Heb. 4:16 NKJV)

Point: III. **Surpassing Peace**

Our hope is not in what we can see but in what we can't see. Therefore, our faith is our sight. Our faith then enables us to endure and fight the good fight, to stand and not be moved by the world. Even when your journey and the road seem hard, we can be confident that Jesus will never forsake us or leave us. Paul wrote to the Philippians and told them this:

Being confident of this very thing, that He who has begun a good work in you will complete it until the day of Jesus Christ. (Philippians 4:6-7 NKJV)

Chapter Six

I will close my book with a brief glimpse of a life torn apart by tragedy unspeakable and rebuilt by our loving God Jesus Christ.

In my first book, *From Hate to Love, a Survivor's Story*, I tried to capture the pain and suffering that come from being a child of abuse. In the story, I changed many things to protect my parents from what would be sheer grief. I certainly didn't want that for them nor did I find it necessary to hurt them.

After reading the book, a dear friend of mine suggested I write a sequel explaining my deliverance by Jesus in what seems to be a story very similar to that of the Apostle Paul. However, when it happened to me, I didn't even know one verse in the Bible. I didn't know Jesus was actually personal, and I certainly didn't know Paul existed. So with an open mind and a clear heart, I will tell you many segments of my adult life to give you a clearer understanding of just how important you are to God and why He loves you so much.

My teen years were spent in absolute confusion about the "God" of my grandparents and the "God" of some well meaning Christians. My step-mother's (mom as I grew to know her) parents were "old school" and very Old Testament. "Spare the rod and spoil the child," comes to mind often when I tried to reconcile the abuse I took. Questions like, how could a loving God allow such horrible treatment in the name of God and all that is good? Let's examine the well meaning Christians of my teen years.

For the most part, these were people that we look at and thought things like: *They are good people; they don't bother anyone and seem real nice and attend a church service.* I am certain you get the idea here. Well the problem with that was I was trying to filter good things through a destroyed mind and very hurt emotions.

For example, pornography was everywhere in my life since I was five years old. The late sixties and early seventies were full of baby sitters that my parents hired that had open sex with their boyfriends, and drugs were common to my culture. So as I got older, these practices became the norm for me. To say the least, I was not shocked by them even if I chose one over the other.

At about sixteen, I thought I would have to really clean up my act in order for God to notice me. I would have to stop doing one thing and start doing another.

Okay, so try stopping drugs and sex on your own after years of use. To fill in the gap, sexual activity with a female partner started at thirteen and the alcohol and marijuana started at fourteen. Both, as any addict has discovered, are very attractive and mind consuming. I simply couldn't stop so I set the whole God idea aside as some sort of life for others to have but not me.

At twenty, I was in my very first full time career as an insurance agent for a moderate sized life insurance company. My district manager was of the Catholic faith and wine drinking was totally permissible, which I deemed a little closer to myself than the staunch belief that any alcohol is a sin against God. I had a girlfriend who was Catholic and rather promiscuous. I thought, *well, if she is okay with God of that understanding, perhaps I could be also*. My thinking was all wrong at the time. I had something going on I didn't understand or fully grasp at the time.

I had a real curiosity of wanting to know who God really was, where He came from, and why He is paying us any attention? I didn't know to go to the Bible for answers like that. I wasn't brought up with a Bible as any sort of help. In fact, I never even saw one in my home. So for years those questions just remained unanswered.

At twenty, I met a woman who was a nineteen year old college student. We met at a party a client of mine invited me to. It was the drinking kind of party and various drinks were served until you landed on the one you liked. This continued for hours. So this woman and I hit it off and got carried away with each other and spent the night together. A day or so later, I found myself calling her and setting up another date.

In these next few weeks together, I found out that she was Baptist in faith and her whole family was tied to the church. Again, I was confused about the God of Holiness and Purity, considering our behavior was well below that standard. I would later learn that His standards are not to be compared to ours no matter how holy we think we are.

Six months later, we got married and set off on a life full of hope and promise. I was even accepted in the church and asked for membership which was granted me. I was now somebody to someone and was going somewhere all at the same time.

Four months into the marriage, she decided to have an affair with a co-worker. Even though her mom and the pastor wouldn't help me with my thoughts and feelings about that, I stuck it out with her. We never talked about it again. Shortly after, she told me she was pregnant. So now I really needed to stick around to see if the baby was mine or the other guy's. The boy turned out to be mine! Now what should I do? My marriage is falling apart for various reasons like work, trust issues, and lack of communication. I was very alone in all this and pretty sure she chose to ignore it all.

After three years and ten days, she told me to move out, and she filed for divorce. Dejected and alone, I left. Defeated in the only real love I thought could ever exist, promoted the okay to literally abuse every woman in my life for the next two decades.

For the next six months or so, I balanced visitation with my son, girlfriends, work, travel, and the over bearing demands of a sub-regional manager who just had nothing better to do than break-out lectures on his district level managers. Oh, and God was nowhere to be heard of or talked about in my circle of life. Just to let you know, I put that nice new Bible my former wife gave me back in the box it came in and in exactly the same condition I received it, not an underline, highlight, or any other indication that it had even been opened.

My twenty-fifth birthday was spent alone watching re-runs of Miami Vice and drinking cognac. What a miserable existence I was having. I was depressed and beaten again. The girl I was dating ran off with the ring I gave her and some other guy so I decided it was time for a life change.

I had just spent the last seven years selling insurance all over the state of Michigan. Even though I made a tremendous amount of money, I was basically broke. I was a believer in chasing one's dreams so I did just that. From the age of ten, I knew I wanted to be a police officer. In fact, I will describe how I saw that for me: I would be an Illinois State Trooper, have a little white house with a picket fence around it, a wife (with blond hair) and two children who would just love their daddy. Reach for the stars, and if you catch the moon you did pretty well. I say I caught the moon. I quickly resigned my position as the district manager and started planning a move to Illinois.

Once in Illinois and several locations later, I landed in northern Illinois, northwest of the city of Chicago. I did, however, return to insurance with the same company there in order to make ends meet until the police opportunity became available. After months of waiting, a job opportunity opened with the police department. I also began another marriage to a woman I met through my new job.

After six months, the marriage was over and I dove deeper into my new love: police work. There I found a whole new identity and purpose for my life. Of course, God was even more removed from me than ever. Not that God went anywhere, but I sure did. I believed, *if it's gonna be, it's up to me!* So I did just that. I worked harder at being the best patrolman this one horse town had ever had. Three merits of commendation and a reputation as fair without prejudice is what I earned. So the chief, who was an old school lieutenant, suggested I go to a bigger department where my skill could be used more often than the occasional vandalism call. Although, in one year, more stuff was stirred up than in centuries past. So this small town asked me to find another place to stir up stuff.

I did just that. 20 miles south was a town of about five thousand and at least eighteen full-time officers. They had all new equipment and plans to build a new police department complete with three holding cells and a starting salary of $29,000. That was ten thousand more than I made the year before. Needless to say, when I got the call telling me that I was number one on their hire list, and the job was mine if I would accept, I accepted immediately.

January 1992, I started as a patrolman and quickly earned the reputation as an aggressive pursuer of justice. I had the most traffic stops, contacts, and arrests every month. I participated in public safety seminars for the community, was sent to breathalyzer school, and the Reid School of Interrogation. After one year, I was promoted to detective and stayed on for another year.

I met a woman who was a dispatcher. I got very close to her and her family. I felt like things were really taking shape for the dreams I always had. I asked her father if I could marry his daughter who, by the way, was about six years younger than me. He thought the idea sounded good but that we should live together for a year first. Her father figured that if it didn't work out then no loss, just move on. She had never been married and I had already been married twice, so in his thinking the odds were against us.

After six months, we got her parents to agree to a wedding for nine months later. During this time, things were very rocky at work because of the dating or living together of co-workers. That meant that one of us would have to work an opposite shift of the other. During this time, her father was buying the company in which he had been the comptroller for the past twenty years. This meant nothing to us at the time. What mattered to us was our life. So I quite the force and went right back to the insurance industry so I could run my own show, and no one could tell me how to live my life. I never thought I would miss something so much as I did the police work. It was all a horrible experience. Time went by and now her dad was talking with me about coming on board with his company to help him out.

I took him up on his offer, and after six months in the film room (grunt work if you ask me), he promoted me to V.P. of Operations with an emphasis in sales and customer relations. Perfect for me - I was the boss, drank during my lunches, caroused at sporting events, and lived like there was no tomorrow.

There was huge growth in the business, bonuses, travel, and total control over my schedule. What more could a person want? Again, God was of no account to me and certainly I didn't think He cared about a guy like me. Selfish and self-centered was what I was. It was all about me and no one was going to get in the way of what I wanted, not even my wife.

My wife had been working with her mother in a freelance business but now decided it was time to seek out her own dream of being, of all things, a police officer. I was absolutely livid with her! I had given up my dream of being a police officer so she would not have the stress of schedule conflicts, low pay, and the lack of the nicer things. Now she wanted to thumb me and cause me grief; I don't think so! I left her quick and sudden. Of course, I had liquid courage and a girlfriend to help me do it.

I resigned in the wake of "blood is thicker than water" even though her dad found no fault in what I did. That was only because he was concerned about having to go back to work to cover for the lack of me being there.

I want to close this chapter with a brief update of where I was with the whole concept of God. He absolutely didn't want anything to do with me. Of course, that was only my opinion based on what others had told me about Him. I was under the very distinct impression that if I couldn't get my life straight, then God didn't want me. Also, I had a lot of fast and loose opinions about God from the Catholic faith such as: go to church (Mass) on the holidays, and say some prayers to Mary and you're good for another year or so. These false assumptions were only based on those peoples' thoughts that were in my life. What a mess I was in and didn't even know it.

Chapter Seven

I want to start by saying that as far as the world was concerned, I was just living life. You know there is nothing unusual about being married multiple times and living life to gain all you can at any price. The corporate climbs are based on: step on your competition, get to the next level promotion, or survival of the fittest. Those are all really a self-centered motive and never about the other person and their needs.

I hung around Northern Illinois for about ten months and dabbled in real estate. I even married the girlfriend who helped me end my last marriage. It was the least I could do since I had no identity outside of another person. She just happened to be my next identity. The demands were high as she was spoiled rotten by her mom and certainly didn't have any respect for money. That thought was kind of lame coming from me, someone who gambled, drank, and spent hundreds of dollars in a weekend on prostitutes.

This relationship had, "You do for me and I will do for you," written all over it. Simple math is what I told a friend once. I let her keep all the money she earned in a part time retail job, threw a few hundred in for good measure, didn't complain about what she bought, and we would get along just fine. This went on for at least five years as we went in and out of marriage.

We left Illinois in search of warmer climate and ended up in Charlotte, North Carolina. I took a job with one of my old customers from my previous career but he ended up being bankrupt by the time I started. No loss, I went to another old customer and landed a sales position in a very successful home improvement company that specialized in windows for homes.

This career promised excellent earnings, and I excelled quickly. After getting the rhythm down, I was back to drinking and gambling my entire commission checks away. After making friends with a man who was returning to work following a car accident, a new plan was being thought of. Not my plan but his. Our sales numbers were excellent and very similar each month as he tracked them. After eight months for me, and four months for him, he suggested we become partners in a franchise. This came on the eve of my trying to decide if I would stay in the business at all.

I agreed, and in December 1999, we signed our franchise agreement and moved to Chattanooga TN. We were off and running January 7, 2000. Success came easy. By September, I had sold 1 million dollars of gross sales, and my part of the initial investment was paid back and salaries went to 100k each. We grew by leaps and bounds and had taken over Georgia. Atlanta became another hub for us.

We hired and trained sales reps in TN and GA., had mail rooms in Nashville and Knoxville, TN. We also planned to start in Alabama the following year. By mid 2001, we had six reps in two states selling 2 million net at a 40% profit margin. Our personal income was around $150K plus benefits.

I failed to mention my friend was a religious man when we first met. Well, that is what I called him anyway because I was invited to visit him at church one Sunday before leaving Charlotte. After arriving in Chattanooga, we were to meet at a Presbyterian church, but we were late. He felt that we would be looked at badly so we never returned or sought out any other church to attend. Let me also clarify that I found yet another identity in this person, not self, nor in God.

Putting religion aside, we worked like mad men to develop more territory and bigger pay checks. We often times worked through the night planning where to go next. Of course, we justified all this in the name of what was good for our families. His family consisted of a wife and two adopted children from her first marriage and a son he had back in Charlotte. I was married and had a dog.

In 2002, business was so booming that even our families were of no consequence to lose in the name of success. That is exactly what started to unfold - divorces and shattered lives. He decided that he needed to be free of the attachment of a demanding wife and kids who wanted their father's attention. He hired a nineteen year old secretary and groomed her to replace the wife and kids. She fell right into the flash of big money and power over others very quickly.

I was not interested in my wife, again a non emotional relationship, but became very interested in my married secretary. She was not married when we hired her, and shortly I took her on as the secretary of the finance department which I ran along with all inside personnel and the sales team.

My days were consumed with travel and training new reps or updating the current reps to changes in the market place. This secretary and I spent hours a day on the phone. As I travelled and worked deals, she would ask me about them before sending them to get bought. Conversations turned personal nearly every time. I was starting to need a person to confide in and dump my needs on. The massage parlors were just as lonely as my bedroom at home most times. Of course, this was wrong on every level, but I didn't care about right or wrong. I only cared about my needs being met. At that time, if you asked me about God, I would say, "What concern is that of mine?"

My business partner separated from his wife in 2002. After several months of him telling me my wife was nothing but a gold digger, I separated from her in 2003. After this, we launched into a whole new realm of success. I had managed to stay sober for 365 days, but on the 366th day, I celebrated by drinking and I never looked back.

My conscious had become seared and cold, and I abandoned morality altogether. Wild and careless is what I became.

By October of 2003, I was fried. I was over worked and tired of it all. I needed a break and badly. So I reached out to Charlotte, North Carolina to help me. I will call her Charlotte for the sake of privacy.

Chapter Eight

The thought of starting over didn't bother me as much as the, *I got screwed over* attitude. Revenge became a new term and goal of my life. This began an intense hate for people that I thought I trusted with my life. Suddenly my childhood and all the evil I had endured came roaring back with such intensity that I began to fantasize about killing my own parents for what they had done to me and Marla.

This attitude and intensity propelled me through my thirties and into my early forties. The cycle of drinking, drugging, and self-centeredness only increased and in its wake left many innocent people hurt and destroyed.

I began my DUI arrest cycle in Panama City Beach, Florida in the spring of 2004, and would have another in 2005 and 2006 in Tennessee. The whole time I only felt hate for the reason I was this way and really didn't care anymore about life or living it.

However, I wasn't quite ready to kill myself as I was about to in 2003. No, this time I had a point to make and the optimistic attitude of, *I can go on one more time.* So I got married again in hopes that I would find some sort of reason to exist beyond hate. Just to get out of bed every day, I used to encourage myself with the thought that another marriage would give me purpose for sure. I was not trying to feel sorry for myself. I was pathetic and that is just the truth.

I say pathetic because I had options to get help. Sure, I could have checked back into treatment like before, although, I would have to get honest with what was really going on with me, or the best treatment wasn't going to help. This is true for any one. My excuse was that I didn't want to show weakness or be perceived as weak. And yes, I thought that even seeking the God of my understanding, as AA teaches, was still a weakness I wasn't willing to admit.

I did find someone to marry who had three children from three different relationships of her own. Perfect, this woman is as messed up as I am. That was only a deep internal realization, not one openly discussed. So as I got deeper into this marriage, I was told that she wanted us to have dominate and submissive relationship. I won't linger on this point only to say it didn't work for me. I was supposed to be the dominate role and she would take orders and do as she was told. The payoff for her was to be beaten if she disobeyed. She wanted this and I couldn't do it because I was too weak.

The alternative would prove worse. I became an abused spouse. This is very hard for any man to admit on any level. When we drank and partied, she would get angry and beat me with her fist and abuse me sexually. I was also made to participate in sexual acts with her and others as she saw fit. This went on for nearly three years and increased with intensity each time.

I became afraid and enraged that I wasn't in control of my life at any level. The flash-backs of sexual assault from my abusers came rushing back time and again with more frequency and intensity. I was absolutely lost and had nowhere to turn. Oh, I did try the pastor of a local church and asked him to pray for me, but that was pretty much a desperate way to relieve some sort of guilt. Guilt is really what I thought of most the time. I was in some way convinced that this whole life of mine was my fault, and no doubt much of it was.

Who I was to God was the farthest thing from my mind. Again, I said I couldn't join the "Christian club" since I couldn't stay sober enough to make it to the church. Besides, what would God want with an immoral heathen like me anyway? I was convinced that Gad was just waiting to smash me.

I assure you this is a horrible place to be emotionally or mentally, but what's a man to do who grew up believing what he was told as a child. If you can relate, please dump that entire negative reservoir, and know that Jesus isn't that way at all. In fact, He is just loving you and waiting for you to give Him a chance to prove just how much.

Chapter Nine

My salvation didn't come by way of a church service, a witness on the street, or any other "normal" way. It was June 6, 2008, on a Friday evening. I found myself in trouble with the law once again. But I swore as before, *I wasn't going back to jail for any reason,* so I ran.

I had been drinking since 10 AM and it was now about 5:30 in the evening. As experienced in drinking as I was, I knew I was about .24 blood alcohol content or, in other words, just over twice the legal limit.

I wasn't being chased by any one when I tried to climb the very large hill that led to the highway below the other side. The hill was full of tall grass, saplings, and brier bushes which I still carry the scars from. I fought to climb this hill, cursing and complaining about all the injustice in my life. I was only determined to get to the other side and to the highway which I thought for sure would lead to freedom.

Half way up the hill, I was suddenly grabbed in my chest, picked up and thrown down the hill into the creek at the bottom. Now I didn't roll down as though I was clumsy; I was lifted off my feet and thrown. Stunned and angrier now I said, "Oh, no you don't, I am going up this hill." Again, half way up, freedom just over the other side, Wham! Again, hit in the chest, picked up, and thrown to the bottom of the hill. Again, I insisted I must get to the other side and nothing will stop me. Wham! A third time I was hit in the chest, picked up, and thrown down the hill into the creek.

I gave up on the hill and snuck through some yards to my attorney's paralegal secretary's home. Wet and confused about what had just taken place, I knocked on their garage door. Hearing voices from inside I said, "Hey its Rob I need to talk to you now!" The door opened and I slid under it to find cover faster.

I must have looked like I just came from a cat fight. I was bleeding from my arms and legs and soaking wet. After asking for a beer and a cigarette which they gladly gave me, I rambled on about being accused of a heinous crime. She asked what she could possibly do to help. I responded, "Get my attorney on the phone; he can help." She called and talked to him for about a minute and didn't even let me explain to him what was going on, but hung up and called the police to see if they were looking for me. In just minutes, four squad cars pulled up in front of her house. With guns drawn, they took me into custody. What a mess!

Once at the police department, the detective asked if I wanted to make a statement. I responded in very short tone, "No, not without counsel." He said he thought I would say that and turned me over to a patrolman to transfer me to the county jail. I knew of this patrolman and he seemed to be reasonable so I didn't feel as though I would endure any questions from him.

In conversation, he stated that if I would just hang in there, things could work out for the good. I had no idea what he meant and how he could say that and mean it? I knew from being a former police officer that I had a long haul ahead of me, and my track record wouldn't help any. Once at the county building, he gave me what would prove to be my last smoke and then led me inside.

I was utterly amazed that at this late hour on a Friday night, there was only one other man in the drunk tank. Not only that, but the booking process was way beyond normal and everyone seemed so pleasant and not cruel or insensitive as I had found in my past arrest.

After appearing before the magistrate and hearing my bond was $25,000 or ten percent, I made one feeble attempt to call someone for help but to no avail. I was on my own. So they transferred me to the property room where I had to surrender all personal items and clothing to put on an orange jump suit and green socks. From there, they took me to the fifth floor, east 2.

Once inside the double steel doorways that slid open with quite the loud clank, I was led to the middle cell and instructed to get on the top left bunk. I heard a voice in the dimly lit room say, "It will be okay." Later I found out that was "pops" as he was referred to by most inmates. Pops slept on the lower right bunk and rarely got up except to eat and take meds. I was convinced the meds were the reason he could sleep entire days away as though they didn't exist.

I crawled up to the bunk and quickly fell into some very deep sleep as though I hadn't slept in weeks or maybe months. Saturday came and went, and I didn't even know it. In fact, I have no memory of Saturday at all even to this day. Saturday just didn't exist somehow. I figure I probably slept through it and who would care inside the jail any way?

Sunday morning 5 AM, the guards opened the doors to let us out for chow. There were 3 four men cells and a small area to sit at metal tables to eat and or gather around for various games the guys would play. So small was the room that 12 men could not stand shoulder to shoulder in a straight line. The line was hooked at the end like the letter "J".

I was the last one in line and there were men to my right side and the empty cells to my left. The noise was loud and came from various cell blocks down the guard's walk. It was hard to tell since it echoed off the metal walls, and everyone seemed to talk over the other. I wasn't quite sure what exactly was going on with me, other than, it seemed like days ago I had arrived, and I was definitely in jail.

In just minutes of standing there, the room seemed to get quiet and the lighting adjusted to enclose me. I heard a voice say, "Look on the floor behind you". I mean this was so audible that I thought someone was standing behind me and said that. I turned my head to the left and looked down on the floor behind me.

I immediately looked back straight and not at all knowing what I saw. I turned back again to see if I might have imagined it. Nope, it was still there. It was a crushed down body which looked like something you would see Wile E. Coyote look like after being smashed by a large boulder.

This body had an oversize head with blacked out eye sockets and a face. I saw that it was me. I was the dead guy. Just at the moment of recognizing this, I was looking straight forward again and heard, "I can put you back in there or you are going to come with Me." I was obviously blown away and could only surmise that God was talking to me directly. I didn't say a word but responded to God quietly in my heart.

I went back to sleep for a few hours. When I got up, I started looking for a Bible. That seemed like the most natural thing to do. As you might remember, I had no understanding of who God was, is, or what He could possibly want with me. I didn't know His word or any one in His Word. All I knew at this moment was I needed to read and discover what was happening to me.

The experience was so awesome that I dedicated the day to reading His word and every day since. I stopped to pray, which was full of questions, tears, and sobbing before Him. I didn't care who heard me; I had to seek God's face. I wanted to know Him intimately. This was a very different feeling than what

I had ever experienced before. I just had to understand what was going on.

As time went by in jail, the world just seemed to disappear and I was getting to know something of God's grace. I was a pretty sick person on every level of life: Physically - because in 2005, I was diagnosed with severe bipolar. In 2006, I was diagnosed with emphysema which progressed to several bouts of pneumonia and bronchitis since I wouldn't stop smoking. Mentally - because I was battered and abused and wouldn't trust anyone for anything. Emotions were off the chart. And my spiritual was non-existent.

Other things were now taking place that I didn't expect. When I was arrested, I was bleeding from my arms and legs due to the brier bushes. I was without my medication for the bipolar disorder. The guys told to put in a request to see the doctor, so I did, but no answer came. One of the men had some Noxzema cream and let me use it to put on my sores. Others were offering me some food they bought on commissary.

I stopped watching TV and reading anything secular. Instead, I started to write what was happening to me. Then out of the blue, the jail chaplain requested that I visit with him. Bill was a devout Christian and believed God could and would do miracles in peoples' lives if only they would let Him.

About the second visit or so, I told Bill what had happened the morning of June 8, to see what he would have to say about it. His reaction was not what I had anticipated. He was moved and very supportive. He asked me to tell him everything. Over the next several visits, I was able to tell him the short version of my life and all that God was doing for me. These were exciting times!

On one visit with Bill, he suggested that I write a cleansing letter of forgiveness to those who had abused me. He explained that it could help in giving me closure. Since there was no requirement to send them out, I could destroy them as God destroyed the hurt from my past life. The letters were easier than I thought and flowed well as the Spirit lead me to write.

I gave them to Bill to read. He was amazed of the clarity and descriptive nature of the writing. Bill asked to use them, after taking out the names, so that it could be a model for others to use for clarity. They are still being used to this day. I said that it must be a Romans 8:28 purpose because that was a lot of pain to see so much good come from them.

Today, I am free in Jesus from every sort of bondage from my past life. The things which I have shared with you from my past such as addictions, hate, revenge, selfishness, un-forgiveness, and anger are gone – I have been set free. God has made me a new creation. The old things are gone and the new has come! That isn't just some nice thing to say; it is an everyday existence in Christ. I am living everyday in the victory over the darkness which had blinded and ruled over me!

Let me be clear in saying that the world is out to get you, because Satan is running the world around us for now. The day is coming, and soon, that Jesus will descend and split the Eastern Sky wide open and take His family home.

I in Christ am free from the slavery or ownership the world used to have over me and still has over those outside of Jesus. I am no longer enticed by what the world has to offer. Again, this isn't something we do by getting a grip on our emotions, habits, or thoughts. It only happens in Jesus who holds all the power over all things. Blessed be the name of the Lord!

Chapter Ten

Very few people have heard my testimony. Not that I don't want to shout from the tallest mountain about the awesomeness of God who raised this dead man from the dominion of the underworld; I only do so with the Spirits leading.

I was sentenced to prison for the next three and half years, and everyone was saying how I was so "lucky." I say blessed beyond measure. In addition, I was to receive a full and complete exam by two doctors and a psychiatrist. These took place at the first prison. I was given chest x-rays, and blood test upon blood test. There was nothing wrong with me - no lung issues, no kidney problems, no nervous shakes, and no psychiatric needs to treat. Praise God, I was completely healed and in my right mind. Many other favors of God came upon me and the new life I live is only praise to Him and not of anything I could have done or ever would have done.

The most amazing thing in all this is that you can plainly see that God is no respecter of persons. What

He wants is a broken and contrite heart laid open to Him so that He can lavish Himself into that person and their existence. So will you let Him?

There is an overwhelming change in store for the one who seeks God for who He is and not for what He can give you. Oh, He wants to give you so many things that are for your good, but first He wants to give you a new birth. He wants your heart; He wants to give you a new life.

I know that every promise of God is yes and amen in Christ Jesus. And the most important promise is, "Christ in you the hope of glory," Col. 1:27. This is the promise that Jesus will live in you by His Spirit, empowering you to overcome all the old ways of living, to provide you with all that is needed to conquer sin and live in a new way of life. Paul told the church in Philippi, "I can do all things in Christ who strengthens me". There are so many more promises for you to search the Scriptures for.

As I close this book, it is my prayer that you will have a new and deeper understanding of who you are to God and what you truly mean to Him. That you would find the peace of God that surpasses all understanding. Be blessed in the Lord my brothers and sisters.

So in summary, God is no respecter of persons, and what He has done for me, He can do for you as well. Please enjoy your new life in Jesus.